Sir Arthur Evans

Frontispiece:
Sir Arthur Evans. 1932
Reproduced courtesy the British Academy

Cover:
Sir Arthur Evans among the Ruins of the Palace of Knossos, by Sir William Blake Richmond, R.A., (1842-1921)
Presented to the Ashmolean Museum by an International Body of Subscribers in 1907

UNIVERSITY OF OXFORD · ASHMOLEAN MUSEUM

SIR ARTHUR EVANS 1851-1941
'A Memoir' by D.B. Harden

ASHMOLEAN MUSEUM OXFORD 1983

Text and illustrations
© Ashmolean Museum, Oxford 1983
All rights reserved
ISBN 090009 086 3

Ashmolean Museum Publications
Archaeology, History & Classical Studies

Treasures of the Ashmolean
Ancient Cyprus
Ancient Egypt
Ancient Iran
Ancient Iraq
Ancient Italy
Archaeology, Artefacts and the Bible
The Arundel Marbles
Greek Vases
Greek Terracottas
Scythian Treasures in Oxford
Arthur Evans and the Palace of Minos

Designed by Peter Miller
and printed in Great Britain by Reedprint Ltd., Windsor,
Berkshire, 1983
Set in 9pt Century Textbook Light

Foreword

Arthur Evans was the Department's greatest benefactor and its present standing owes more to him than any other man. Donald Harden, who was the Assistant Keeper of the Department of Antiquities from 1929 to 1945 and Keeper from 1945 to 1956, and who thus came to know Arthur Evans well during the last years of his life, tells of his active and successful career on the basis of his own vivid memories and those of many older contemporaries.

Humphrey Case, Keeper of Antiquities, Ashmolean Museum

Acknowledgements

In the compilation of this memoir constant recourse has been had to Dr. Joan Evans's *Time and Chance, the Story of Arthur Evans and his Forebears*, published by Longmans, Green and Co., London, in 1943. Help was also derived from obituaries of Sir Arthur Evans in *Obituary Notices of Fellows of the Royal Society*, III, no.10 (Dec. 1941), 941-68 (with copious bibliography), in the *Proceedings of the British Academy*, XXVII (1942), 323-57, and in the *Dictionary of National Biography, Supplement 1941-50* ed. L.G. Wickham-Legg and E.T. Williams (1959), 240-3, all by (Sir) John Myres; as well as from two other obituaries, one by Sir John Forsdyke, the other unsigned, but undoubtedly by E.T. Leeds, in *The Antiquaries Journal*, XXII (1942), 69-73. Further light on Sir Arthur's life and work may also be sought in J.J. Wilkes, 'Arthur Evans in the Balkans 1875-81' in the *Bulletin of the Institute of Archaeology, University of London*, 13 (1976), 25-56, and in Sylvia L. Horwitz, *The Find of a Lifetime, Sir Arthur Evans and the Discovery of Knossos* (The Viking Press, New York, and Weidenfeld and Nicolson, London, 1981).

The frontispiece of this memoir, from a photograph by Elliott & Fry, Ltd., has been reproduced by courtesy of the British Academy. Plate 23 has been reproduced by kind permission of Youlbury Scout Camp.

I would also like to express my grateful thanks to Mrs Ann Brown, Dr. Roger Moorey and Mr. Michael Vickers for assisting me in the preparation of this revised edition of my memoir.

D.B.Harden

Introduction

Arthur Evans was not only a consummate scholar, historian and archaeologist; he was a man of great and abiding determination who rarely failed, however long it might take, to reach his goal. Apart from the worldwide acclaim he received because of his long years of work on the Minoan civilization of Crete, his own University of Oxford must ever be in his debt for the immense drive with which, from the time he became Keeper of the Ashmolean Museum in 1884, he set about revivifying the Museum, changing it from a collection of curios into a modern museum of art and archaeology, and forcing it during his Keepership through successive stages of building, reorganization and development, when, and after, it moved from the Old Ashmolean Building in Broad Street (now the Museum of the History of Science) to its new home in Beaumont Street in 1894.

After his death in 1941 the *Report of the Visitors of the Ashmolean Museum* for that year recorded how 'Almost every section has, at various times, received valuable additions by the gift of a large part of his own collections or of those of his father, Sir John Evans, and frequent monetary donations have marked the whole period of well-nigh sixty years of close association with the Museum... In addition to these he has bequeathed funds for the upkeep, both of the Minoan Room... and of the Heberden Coin Room'.

The first edition of this memoir was published in connexion with an exhibition held in the Museum in 1951 to celebrate the centenary of Sir Arthur Evans's birth. The objects then exhibited, except for three oil paintings from the Department of Fine (now Western) Art, were drawn from the collections of the Department of Antiquities, and represented material excavated or otherwise acquired by Sir Arthur Evans during the course of his amazingly long life as an archaeologist and traveller. Some of those obtained by him during his earliest years came to the Museum amongst his father Sir John Evans's collections of Anglo-Saxon and European Dark Age material (presented by Arthur Evans in 1908) or amongst his father's collections of prehistoric and Roman antiquities (presented by Sir Arthur in 1927). The remainder were presented by him or purchased for the Museum by him from time to time, before, during and after his tenure of the Keepership from 1884-1908.

Taken together these represented a most varied group of interests — coins of Sicily, the Balkans, the Roman Empire and medieval days, Renaissance and modern medals, Roman and medieval antiquities from Oxford and neighbourhood, gem-stones from the Balkans and Crete, Greek vases and terracottas, Minoan antiquities from Knossos, Roman sculpture, Spanish material of El Argar and earlier cultures, and many other things. There is, indeed, scarcely a single section of the collections in the Department of Antiquities which was not enriched in some degree through his agency, and the Department of Western Art also benefited from his generosity.

Now, thirty-one years after the 1951 exhibition, when the Arthur Evans Room in the museum has been redesigned through the generosity of the Amey Roadstone Corporation Fund and the Sir Arthur Evans Bequest Fund to house a fresh display of the Cretan (Minoan), Mycenaean and Cycladic antiquities, a revised edition seems appropriate. It is hoped that even without the fuller visual evidence available in the 1951 exhibition, the memoir will demonstrate clearly and intelligibly the main facets of what, during his long life, Sir Arthur Evans was able to accomplish for archaeology in general and for Oxford archaeology and his beloved Ashmolean Museum in particular.

Arthur John Evans 1851-1941

Arthur John Evans, the eldest son of John Evans (later Sir John Evans, K.C.B.) and Harriet Evans (*née* Dickinson), was born at Nash Mills, Hemel Hempstead, Herts., on 8 July 1851. His formal education took place at Harrow and Brasenose College, Oxford, where he graduated in December 1874 with First Class Honours in the newly-founded School of Modern History. His father, John Evans, was by this time one of the foremost archaeologists and numismatists in England, and Arthur showed from early boyhood a genius for and interest in coins and antiquities of all kinds. His home background thus prepared the way for his long and distinguished archaeological career. It was not merely passive preparation. Before he left school Arthur had made several archaeological journeys both in England and abroad in his father's company, and had learnt to collect objects and assess their interest and importance. While at Oxford, too, he published one numismatic paper, collected antiquities from building operations in the city and from sites such as that of the Romano-Celtic temple at Woodeaton, near Oxford, and read at least two papers before the Oxford Architectural and Historical Society.

The seven years (1875-82) following his graduation Arthur Evans spent mainly in archaeological research and travel in the Balkans, basing himself on Ragusa (Dubrovnik). He soon developed a deep interest in Balkan politics and Slav freedom movements, and, becoming a correspondent of the *Manchester Guardian*, had much to do with explaining Balkan political aspirations to the British Government and public. These activities ultimately led to his imprisonment by the Austrians in Ragusa in 1882 (Pl. 1) and, although released after six weeks, he was banished the country and it was many years before he could return. He and his wife Margaret (daughter of E.A. Freeman, the historian), whom he had married in 1878, had to leave their house, the Casa San Lazzaro in Ragusa, and return to England to seek a new home and a new sphere of activity.

During his time in the Balkans Evans had fortunately paid nearly as much attention to archaeology as to politics and had collected many things, especially coins and gems, and a great deal of archaeological information (Pl. 2). The results, published in his *Antiquarian Researches in Illyricum* and elsewhere, and a knowledge of general archaeology and history derived from his early training, made him a fitting candidate for the post of Keeper of the Ashmolean Museum. This fell vacant on J.H. Parker's resignation in 1884, and Arthur Evans was appointed to succeed him on 8 June.

In the earlier years of the 19th century the Ashmolean had made some mark as a centre of teaching in the natural sciences. But the virtual completion of the University Museum in Parks Road in 1860 took all the natural science exhibits from the Ashmolean, while about the same time the books, manuscripts and coins were transferred from the Ashmolean to the Bodleian Library, so that all that remained were the archaeological and ethnographical exhibits, including what had survived of the founder's collections of the 17th century, and a few pictures. One floor of the building, too, had become an examination hall.

The Museum, therefore, needed a strong guiding hand and a forceful personality at its head, if it was to be resuscitated into a worthwhile institution. It found both in Arthur Evans. His policy for the Museum was set out in his inaugural lecture delivered in November 1884, entitled *The Ashmolean Museum as a Home of Archaeology in Oxford.* He soon ousted examiners and examinees and obtained the use of the whole building in Broad Street for museum purposes. He approached the distinguished collector Charles Drury Edward Fortnum, who had already indicated that he was ready and anxious to give his fine collection of classical and medieval art to Oxford, and ultimately obtained the whole of Fortnum's collection, first by arranging loans and gifts, and, finally, through a bequest which included not only objects but also munificent endowments. He also, by his flair for choosing the right thing and keeping contact with the right archaeological workers at home and abroad, rapidly expanded the collections, especially on the Egyptian, Greek and Roman sides, until they were transformed from mere groups of museum objects into a first class medium for teaching and research. Typical of this flair was his acquisition some years later of part of an important tomb-group from (Professor) John Garstang's excavations at Abydos in 1906. The group included a Cretan bridge-spouted vase of polychrome ware of Middle Minoan style and was recognized by Evans as a piece of evidence of primary importance for Cretan chronology (Pl. 3).

Evans's efforts in building up the collections were greatly assisted by his good fortune in starting this drive at the very time when British archaeological endeavour in the eastern Mediterranean countries (and notably in Egypt) was beginning to expand greatly, with societies, institutions, and individual scholars all becoming active in this field of research. There were, therefore, so many opportunities for Evans to acquire the accessions he was seeking that eight years after he took office it was plain that the Broad Street building no longer provided adequate space. Expansion was, of course, impossible on that site. Evans was thus able to press for another stage in his plan — the combination in one building in Beaumont Street of the Ashmolean material and the other main archaeological collections belonging to the University, which had already found a home there in the University Galleries. By arrangement with the Curators of the Galleries and helped by a donation of £10,000 from C.D.E. Fortnum, Evans was able to persuade the University to build an extension to the Galleries on the north, large enough to house the Department of Classical Archaeology under its Professor, Percy Gardner, on the ground floor and the Ashmolean material on the first floor. By the end of 1894, only ten and a half years after he became Keeper, the building was finished and the move had taken place. Evans, with Fortnum's help had, in effect, re-founded the Ashmolean Museum.

His wife Margaret, who had been in poor health for some time, died in March 1893, just when Evans was buying land on Boars Hill near Oxford on which to build a home near enough to the Ashmolean and yet away from the relaxing air of Oxford itself. Grief-stricken as he was, he, characteristically, did not alter his building plans, and his move to the new house, Youlbury took place in the same year as the move of the Ashmolean to Beaumont Street. Youlbury remained his home, and Boars Hill and its amenities one of his major cares and considerations from then until his death in 1941. The house was destroyed in 1950.

During the ten years 1884-1894 Evans's own archaeological work centred mainly on numismatics and British (especially Iron Age) antiquities. As a result of this research he published articles on the Rollright Stones (1895), on the Aesica brooch (1897), and on the Late Celtic urnfield at Aylesford (1890), which he partly excavated (Pl. 4). He also excavated in 1885, but did not publish until 1897, the Roman villa at Frilford, near Oxford. At the same time he continued to travel widely. On visits to Sicily in 1888 and subsequently he was able to acquire for the Museum a number of very fine Greek vases mainly from the site of Gela (Pls. 5,6). His interest in that island was also shown by his publication in 1889 and 1891 of important studies on Sicilian coins: *The 'Horsemen' of Tarentum* (Pl. 7) and *Syracusan 'Medallions'*.

He was at the same time developing a keen interest in the newly discovered Mycenaean civilization of Greece, and more particularly in its scripts — the existence of which he was one of the first, if not the very first, to recognize — and was looking towards Crete as the home of an earlier facet of that same civilization. These studies and these hopes were placed before the public in his 'Primitive pictographs and a prae-Phoenician script from Crete and the Peloponnese' published in the *Journal of Hellenic Studies* in 1894. In that same year he went to Crete to prospect for further evidence in support of his views and to endeavour to acquire the key site, Knossos, for excavation. Acquisition of the site — there were several proprietors — proved difficult and he succeeded, at that time, in buying only one quarter of it. For this and other reasons his desire to begin excavating Knossos was destined to be disappointed for six more years, but the time was not wasted. During several journeys in successive years he built up his knowledge of the island and its antiquities and also laid the foundation of his unrivalled collection of Minoan gem-stones (Pls. 8,9), many of which he found in use as charms by the inhabitants and was obliged, therefore, to inveigle out of their owners by persuasion (chiefly financial).

Finally, early in 1900, after Crete had in 1898 been freed from Turkish domination, Evans acquired the remainder of the site of Knossos and obtained permission from the High Commissioner, Prince George of Greece, to excavate there and on other sites. The task at Knossos was a vast one and it and the publication of its results became his chief care for the remainder of his life.

Excavation began on 23 March 1900 (Pls. 10,11). The major work was concentrated in the first six seasons, 1900-5 (Pl. 13), but there was scarcely a year between 1900 and 1914 and between 1922 and 1939 (Pl. 14) when some work on the site was not undertaken either by Evans himself or by one of his assistants, Duncan Mackenzie, John Pendlebury, Richard W. Hutchinson and the architects, Theodore Fyfe, Christian Doll and Piet de Jong (Pl. 15). As a direct result of these excavations the Ashmolean came to have the finest collection of Minoan antiquities outside Crete itself (Pls. 16,17,19,21).

The excavations were fruitful from the very start. A week after excavations began in 1900 a cache of tablets inscribed in Minoan linear script was found, thus realizing Evans's highest hopes of discovering inscribed material (Pl. 19), and by the end of the year's work it was clear that he had found the headquarters of a new civilization which far transcended both in antiquity of origin and in artistic and cultural stature the Mycenaean of Greece as revealed by Schliemann and others. Many more finds of remarkable quality were unearthed in subsequent years, so that by 1906 Evans knew that the years of work that lay ahead of him at Knossos were numerous. To lessen the stress of working there Evans in that year commissioned Christian Doll to build him a comfortable home near the site. This, the Villa Ariadne, was completed before the year ended (Pl. 20).

Throughout the first six seasons at Knossos Evans also succeeded in taking his share, albeit not always perhaps his full share (as he would have been the first to confess), in running the Ashmolean. Although he had the able support of his Assistant Keeper, C.F. Bell, the strain of endeavouring to combine what were virtually two whole-time jobs became too great. He had often thought of resigning the Ashmolean appointment, but the knowledge that he had not yet succeeded in completing the administrative reforms in Beaumont Street which he considered necessary held his hand.

The year 1908, however, saw the completion of those reforms, by which the three separately controlled departments — the Ashmolean proper, the University Galleries and the Department of Classical Archaeology — were amalgamated administratively under one Board of Visitors of the Ashmolean Museum of Art and Archaeology. In the same year Evans inherited rich legacies from his father and his cousin, and he was thus at last ready to resign his Keepership in order to devote his whole time to his Cretan work. This he did in December 1908, and was succeeded by D.G. Hogarth. Evans was, at the same time, appointed Honorary Keeper, with a seat on the Board of Visitors — which he retained by a later University provision until his death — and his indirect work for the Ashmolean and his interest in its fortunes never ceased. This connexion with Oxford was strengthened by his Honorary Fellowship at Brasenose College, which he had held since 1891, and by his appointment in 1909 as Extraordinary Professor of Prehistoric Archaeology. Further appreciation of his services to Oxford and to archaeology had been signalized a year before his resignation, when in 1907 Evans's friends combined to do him honour by presenting to the Ashmolean the portrait of him by Sir William Richmond (Cover).

Between 1909 and 1914 he devoted himself wholeheartedly to the pursuit of his Cretan researches, both by further excavation and by working on the definitive publication of the results. The work of the first six seasons had already been published in preliminary form in successive volumes of the *Annual of the British School at Athens* from 1900 to 1906. In 1909 the first volume of his *Scripta Minoa* appeared. The remainder of his definitive publications proved a longer task than he expected, and the 1914-18 war broke out before any of them could be made ready. Not only was he planning an excavation report proper; he also prepared the plates for an *Atlas of Knossian Frescoes*, which was ultimately published by M. Cameron and M.S.F. Hood in 1967, (cf. Pl. 21), and had in mind a further volume or volumes of *Scripta Minoa*, Vol. 2 of which, edited by Sir John Myres, was published in 1952 and a third volume entitled *Inscriptions in the Minoan Linear Script of Class A*, edited by W.C. Brice from the notes of Sir Arthur Evans and Sir John Myres appeared in 1961.

Meanwhile he received honours of many kinds. Honorary degrees from Dublin and Edinburgh and election as a Fellow of the Royal Society all came in 1901. He was knighted in 1911 and elected President of the Hellenic Society for three years in that same year. This was followed by the Presidencies of the Society of Antiquaries and of the Royal Numismatic Society (both 1914-19) and the British Association (1916-19).

During the war and at the Peace Conference he was able to recapture his Balkan interests for a while by taking part in the discussion leading to the creation of the modern state of Yugoslavia. The friendships cemented then led him in 1932 to revisit Ragusa and his 1882 prison, and to his being welcomed with great honour by the Yugoslav state as a lifelong friend and helper of its cause.

In 1921 the first volume of his monumental *Palace of Minos* at last appeared and was greeted on all sides as a masterpiece of archaeological synthesis. It was not just an excavation report; it provided a solid basis for the future study of the Minoan civilization as a whole. Further volumes, each one not only publishing new material, but also often revising and reorientating Evans's views about material that had appeared in earlier ones, followed in 1928, 1930 and 1935, and an index volume, prepared by his half-sister, Dr (later Dame) Joan Evans, in 1936. All this time, and indeed even afterwards, he or his assistants continued working at Knossos, clearing up disputed points by further test excavations and opening up new ground on the outskirts of the Palace area (Pl. 14). He also continued his work, begun many years before, of restoring the Palace ruins and embellishing them with reconstructions of their architecture and coloured decorations (Pl. 12).

In 1927, to celebrate his 75th birthday that took place in the previous year, a volume of *Essays on Aegean Archaeology,* edited by Stanley Casson, was presented to him by his friends and colleagues. In 1934 there was a further presentation by a group of archaeological admirers, his bust in marble by David Evans.

Even in old age Arthur Evans's mind was too active to be filled with thoughts of Crete alone. He spent much time in planning with the Oxford Preservation Trust to save the amenities of Boars Hill from the speculative builder, and, as part of that programme, constructed the artificial Jarn Mound as a look-out point with a wild-flower garden at its base (Pl. 22). He revived his earlier interest in ancient numismatics, which had never lain very long dormant. He also followed eagerly the archaeological work in progress in the Oxford area at Ditchley, Frilford and elsewhere, and was himself busy studying the lines of ancient tracks and putative Roman roads in the Boars Hill neighbourhood. At the same time he took a keen interest in Scouting and made over part of his Youlbury estate in perpetuity to the Boy Scouts Association for camping and training activities (Pl. 23).

The beginning of the Second World War found Evans in his 89th year. He had had a serious operation in 1938, but even that did not tie him to his desk or even to his home, and he was travelling abroad in Switzerland only a short time before war broke out. He recovered from a second operation in June 1941 and was able to receive a deputation representing his friends and admirers on his 90th birthday; but he died three days later, on 11 July 1941, ripe in years, ripe in honour and ripe in the affection of all his friends and younger colleagues.

Sir Arthur John Evans, Kt., D.Litt., F.R.S., F.B.A., Hon.V.-P.S.A.
1851-1941

1851-75	**Early Life**
1851	8 July: born at Nash Mills, Hemel Hempstead, Hertfordshire. Eldest son of (Sir) John Evans, K.C.B., F.R.S., Hon.V.-P.S.A. (1823-1908), paper manufacturer, archaeologist, numismatist, and collector, and Harriet Ann, *née* Dickinson (1826-58)
1865-70	Harrow School
1866	Visited the Somme gravels with his father; found his first 'palaeolith' *in situ*
1870-74	Brasenose College, Oxford (commoner): B.A. Oxon. with 1st class honours in History
1871	Travelled in Europe with his brother Lewis
	'On a hoard of coins found at Oxford, with some remarks on the coinage of the first three Edwards', *Numismatic Chronicle*, 2 ser. XI (1871), 264-82
1872	Travelled in Balkans with his brother Norman
1873-4	Travelled in Finland and Russian Lapland
1875	April-July: term at Göttingen University
1875-82	**Slav politics and Balkan archaeology**
1875	Travelled with Lewis in Balkans. First visit to Ragusa (now Dubrovnik)
1876	*Through Bosnia and the Herzegovina on foot, during the Insurrection, August and September 1875, with an historical review of Bosnia* (London, Longmans, Green and Co. 1876; 2nd ed., revised and enlarged, 1877)
1877	Balkan correspondent of *Manchester Guardian*
	Excavated large Bronze Age barrow at Canali, near Ragusa
1878	19 September: married Margaret Freeman (1848-93), eldest daughter of the historian, Professor E.A. Freeman
	October-November: with Margaret at Ragusa, setting up house in Casa San Lazzaro
	Illyrian Letters: a revised selection of correspondence from the Illyrian provinces of Bosnia, Herzegovina, Montenegro, Albania, Dalmatia, Croatia and Slavonia, addressed to the Manchester Guardian *during the year 1877* (London, Longmans, Green and Co., 1878)
1878-81	Travel, archaeological research and political intrigue in Balkans
1880	'On some recent discoveries of Illyrian coins', *Numismatic Chronicle*, 2 ser. XX (1880), 269-302

1882   7 March: arrested by Austrians, charged with complicity in Crivoscian insurrection in south Dalmatia and imprisoned in Ragusa jail (Pl. 1)
            23 April: decree of release, and expulsion from Austrian dominions

1883-94   Oxford and Celtic archaeology
1883   January: settled in Oxford
            May-September: travelled in Greece and eastern Balkans. First meeting with Heinrich Schliemann
1884   17 June: elected Keeper of the Ashmolean Museum. Inaugural lecture: *The Ashmolean Museum as a Home of Archaeology in Oxford* (Oxford, 1884). Began replanning the museum in concert with C.D.E. Fortnum. Urges the re-creation of the coin collection within the museum (See 1922)
1885   Excavated Roman villa at Frilford, near Oxford
1885-6   'Antiquarian Researches in Illyricum, I-II and III-IV', *Archaeologia*, XLVIII (1885), 1-105 and XLIX (1886), 1-167 respectively
1886   July: travelled with Margaret in Crimea and Caucasus
            'Recent discoveries of Tarentine terra-cottas', *Journal of Hellenic Studies*, VII (1886), 1-50
1887   Excavated Belgic cemetery at Aylesford, Kent
1888   Scheme adumbrated for new building for Ashmolean Museum behind University Galleries in Beaumont Street
            Visited Sicily
1889   *The 'Horsemen' of Tarentum* (London, Quaritch, 1889; reprinted from the *Numismatic Chronicle*, 3 ser. IX (1889), 1-228)
1890   'On a Late-Celtic urn-field at Aylesford, Kent, and on the Gaulish, Illyro-Italic, and Classical connexions of the forms of pottery and bronze-work there discovered', *Archaeologia*, LII (1890), 315-88
            'Some new artists' signatures on Sicilian coins', *Numismatic Chronicle*, 3 ser. X (1890), 285-310
1891   Elected to an Honorary Fellowship at Brasenose College, Oxford
            Syracusan 'Medallions' and their Engravers (London, Quaritch, 1891; reprinted, with indices, from the *Numismatic Chronicle*, 3 ser. XI (1891), 205-376)
1891-4   Planning and construction of new building for the Ashmolean Museum in Beaumont Street and of Evans's new house, Youlbury, Boars Hill, Oxford

1893	11 March: death of Margaret Evans at Alassio, Italy
	'A Mykênaean treasure from Aegina', *Journal of Hellenic Studies,* XIII (1893), 195-226
1894	Preparation of Rhind Lectures (Edinburgh) on 'Origins of Celtic Art'

1894-1908 Oxford and Crete

1894	Travel and research in Crete. Began to negotiate for site of Knossos and acquired ownership of one quarter of it
	The History of Sicily from the Earliest Times, by E.A. Freeman, Vol. IV, ed. from posthumous MSS. with supplements and notes by A.J. Evans (Oxford, Clarendon Press, 1894)
1895	In Crete, with J.L. Myres (later Wykeham Professor of Ancient History, Oxford and Visitor of the Ashmolean Museum, Oxford). Investigations at Knossos, Psychro, Goulas
	December: Rhind lectures delivered in Edinburgh (never published)
	Cretan Pictographs and Prae-Phoenician script: with an account of a sepulchral deposit at Hagios Onuphrios near Phaestos in its relation to primitive Cretan and Aegean culture (London, Quaritch, 1895; the first part reprinted from 'Primitive pictographs and a prae-Phoenician script from Crete and the Peloponnese', *Journal of Hellenic Studies,* XIV (1894), 270-372)
	'The Rollright Stones and their Folklore', *Folklore,* VI (1895), 6-51
1896	In Crete, negotiating for remainder of site of Knossos. Excavations at Papoura and Psychro
	In letter to *The Academy* in June Evans first used term 'Minoan' to describe Cretan Bronze Age civilization
1897	Travelled in Sardinia and North Africa
	'A Roman villa at Frilford', *The Archaeological Journal,* LIV (1897), 340-354
	'On two fibulae of Celtic fabric from Aesica (Northumberland)', *Archaeologia,* LV (1897), 179-98 (with F. Haverfield)
1898	March: in Crete with D.G. Hogarth, Director of the British School at Athens (who succeeded Evans as Keeper of the Ashmolean on 5 January 1909) and J.L. Myres. Travel in east Crete
	November: Crete freed from Turkish domination
	Further Discoveries of Cretan and Aegean Script with Libyan and Proto-Egyptian Comparisons (London, Quaritch 1898;

reprinted from the *Journal of Hellenic Studies*, XVII (1897), 327-95)

1899   6 March: C.D.E. Fortnum died bequeathing his collection and an endowment to the Ashmolean Museum

1900   Early in year Evans acquired remainder of site of Knossos and, on behalf of the Hellenic Society and the British School at Athens, obtained decree from Prince George of Greece, the High Commissioner, permitting excavation at Knossos and other Cretan sites

23 March-2 June: first season of excavation at Knossos by Evans, assisted by Duncan Mackenzie. Throne Room, many frescoes and many Linear B tablets discovered (Pls. 11,19)

'Knossos. Summary report of the excavations in 1900', *Annual of the British School at Athens*, VI (1899-1900), 1-70; with five further annual reports for 1901-6 in succeeding volumes to volume XI

1901   Second season of excavation at Knossos

Elected Fellow of the Royal Society, received Hon.D.Litt., Trinity College, Dublin, and Hon.LL.D., University of Edinburgh

The Mycenaean Tree and Pillar Cult and its Mediterranean Relations (London, Macmillan, 1901; reprinted from the *Journal of Hellenic Studies*, XXI (1901), 99-204)

1902-5   Third to sixth seasons of excavations at Knossos

1905   April: Archaeological Congress at Athens at which Evans first announced his proposed nine-period division of Minoan Bronze Age civilization

Elected Correspondant de l'Institut, Paris

1906   Villa Ariadne, Knossos, built (Pl. 20)

The Prehistoric Tombs of Knossos: I. The Cemetery of Zafer Papoura, with a comparative note on a Chamber-tomb at Milatos: II. The Royal Tomb of Isopata (London, Quaritch, 1906; reprinted from *Archaeologia*, LIX (1905), 391-562)

Essai de classification des époques de la civilisation minoenne: résumé d'un discours fait au Congrès d'Archéologie à Athènes, 1905 (London, Quaritch, 1906)

1907   December: portrait of Evans by Sir William Richmond, R.A. presented to Ashmolean by a body of subscribers from many countries

1908   The University, by Statute, amalgamated Ashmolean Museum, University Galleries and Department of Classical Archaeology into the Ashmolean Museum of Art and Archaeology under one Board of Visitors

Sir John Evans died (31 May) and also a cousin, Thomas Gordon Dickinson (28 October), both leaving rich legacies to Arthur Evans

December: resigned Ashmolean Keepership and became Honorary (later Perpetual) Keeper, with seat on Board of Visitors. Presented to Ashmolean his father's fine and comprehensive collection of Anglo-Saxon and European early medieval antiquities

1909-41   Youlbury and Knossos

1909	Campaigned as Tariff Reform candidate for one of the two Oxford University parliamentary seats but withdrew before the election
	At Knossos. Excavated Tomb of Double Axes
	House at Youlbury greatly enlarged and embellished and gardens replanned
	Received Royal Gold Medal of the Royal Institute of British Architects
	Scripta Minoa. The Written Documents of Minoan Crete with special reference to the Archives of Knossos, I. The Hieroglyphic and Primitive Linear Classes... (Oxford, Clarendon Press, 1909)
1910	Received Hon. Ph.D., University of Berlin
1911	Awarded knighthood in King George V's Coronation Honours
1911-14	President, Hellenic Society
1914	*The Tomb of the Double Axes and Associated Group, and the Pillar Rooms and Ritual Vessels of the Little Palace at Knossos* (London, Quaritch, 1914; reprinted from *Archaeologia*, LXV (1914), 1-94)
1914-19	President, Society of Antiquaries of London, and *ex-officio* Trustee of the British Museum
1914-19	President, Royal Numismatic Society
1916-19	President, British Association for the Advancement of Science
1917-19	Worked at Youlbury on *Palace of Minos*
	Active in support of proposed Yugoslav kingdom
1920	Visited Sweden to receive Great Gold Medal of the Swedish Society of Anthropology and Geography
1921	*The Palace of Minos. A comparative Account of the successive Stages of the early Cretan Civilization as illustrated by the Discoveries at Knossos*, volume I (London, Macmillan and Co., 1921)
1922	Official opening of Heberden Coin Room in Ashmolean realized Evans's long-standing plan, first propounded in 1884

1922-6	Further excavation and reconstruction at Knossos
1924	Received Hon.D.Litt., University of Cambridge
	Awarded Huxley Memorial Medal of the Royal Anthropological Institute
1925	*'The Ring of Nestor': a Glimpse into the Minoan After-world, and a Sepulchral Treasure ... from Thisbê, Boeotia* (London, Macmillan, 1925; reprinted from the *Journal of Hellenic Studies*, XLV (1925), 1-75)
1926	February: The Chief Scout, Sir Robert Baden-Powell, laid the foundation stone of the Training Centre for Scout leaders at Youlbury, built on a site given by Sir Arthur Evans
	June: Evans, at Knossos, experienced the earthquake of that year
1927	Villa Ariadne and site of Knossos ceded to British School at Athens, with Duncan Mackenzie as curator
	Presented to Ashmolean his father's comprehensive collection of prehistoric and Roman antiquities
	Bought land on Boars Hill to give to Oxford Preservation Trust and began planning Jarn Mound on the site as a look-out point (Pl. 22)
	15 May: official opening of Youlbury Training Centre by Lord Hampton, Chief Commissioner, Boy Scouts Association (Pl. 23)
1928	*Palace of Minos*, volume II
1929	*The Shaft Graves and Bee-hive Tombs of Mycenae and their Inter-relation* (London, Macmillan and Co., 1929)
1930	Awarded Petrie Medal of University of London
	Grand Cross of Order of Phoenix conferred on Evans by the President of the Greek Republic
	Palace of Minos, volume III
	'Some notes on the Arras hoard: inception of *solidus* standard on British model in medallions of Constantius Chlorus', *Numismatic Chronicle*, 5 ser. X (1930), 221-274
1931	At Knossos, Evans excavated the Temple Tomb (Pl. 14)
1932	Received with acclaim in Croatia and Dalmatia. Revisits Ragusa, including Casa San Lazzaro and the prison (see above, *sub anno* 1882)
1933	*Jarn Mound, with its Panorama ... and Wild Garden of British Plants ...* (Oxford, Vincent, 1933) (Pl. 22)
1934	Awarded, as first recipient, the Gold Medal of the Society of Antiquaries of London
	A portrait bust by David Evans (no relation) presented to him by a group of archaeological admirers

1935	Spring: Evans's last visit to Knossos. Received Honorary Citizenship of Candia (Heraklion) with laurel crown. His bust, by a Greek sculptor, unveiled at entrance to site of Palace of Knossos
	May: erected beacon at Youlbury, forming one of a country-wide chain lit by Boy Scouts in celebration of King George V's Silver Jubilee
	Palace of Minos, volume IV
1936	Awarded Copley Medal of the Royal Society
	Organised Cretan exhibit and catalogue entries as part of the Golden Jubilee Exhibition of the British School of Archaeology at Athens at the Royal Academy of Arts, London
	Palace of Minos, Index volume, by Joan Evans
1937	Awarded the Silver Wolf, highest award in the Boy Scout Movement, by the Chief Scout
	Flew to Holland; revisited Göttingen
	Holland and the Dutch. Handbook for the British Contingent, Boy Scouts ... at Vogelenzang, near Haarlem (London, 1937)
	November: rearrangement of Cretan exhibit in Ashmolean Museum began
1938	Completion of main rearrangement of Cretan exhibit, incorporating gift of nearly all Sir Arthur Evans's remaining Cretan antiquities, including his Minoan gems
	Easter: Evans, now in failing health, underwent a serious operation
1939	Elected Foreign Associate of Académie des Inscriptions, Paris
1941	End May: last visit to London
	8 July: 90th birthday. J.L. Myres (Wykeham Professor of Ancient History), R.M. Dawkins (Emeritus Bywater and Sotheby Professor of Byzantine and Modern Greek) and E.T. Leeds (Keeper of the Ashmolean) visited Youlbury to present a scroll from the Hellenic Society and greetings from the British School at Athens and the Ashmolean
	11 July: death of Sir Arthur Evans. By his wish he was buried in Abbot's Langley churchyard, Herts., near his father and mother

Plates

Cover:
Portrait of Arthur Evans by Sir William Richmond, R.A., commissioned by an International Body of Subscribers and presented in 1907 to the Ashmolean. He is shown surrounded by objects from the excavations at Knossos. In the background can be seen a reproduction of the Cupbearer Fresco, found during the first season's work in 1900

Frontispiece:
Sir Arthur Evans, aged 81; he holds in his right hand an electrotype of the gold pendant bearing confronted bees, c. 17th century B.C., from Mallia, Crete, the original now in Heraklion Museum

Facing Acknowledgements:
Sir Arthur Evans at Knossos

Pl. 1   The prison at Ragusa (now Dubrovnik), Dalmatia, where Arthur Evans was imprisoned from 7 March to 23 April 1882 (p. 10)

Pl. 2   Roman marble head of Hermes, obtained, in exchange for 'a fine top hat made by Lock's of St. James' Street, London', by Evans at Narona, Dalmatia, in 1877. Probably from a sarcophagus of the 2nd century A.D. (p. 11). Given to the Museum by Dame Joan Evans, Sir Arthur's half-sister (1974.438)

Pl. 3   A Middle Minoan II bridge-spouted jar (E.3295) and other objects found in Tomb 416 at Abydos, Egypt, XII Dynasty, during (Professor) John Garstang's excavations in 1906 (p. 11)

Pl. 4   Diagram of a grave in the Late Celtic urnfield at Aylesford, Kent (p. 12). Excavated by Evans in 1887. From *Archaeologia*, LII (1890), 318, fig. 1

Pl. 5   Attic red figure lekythos from Gela attributed to the Pan Painter, c.480 B.C. Nike (p. 12). Acquired by Arthur Evans (1888.1401)

Pl. 6   Attic red figure stamnos from Gela attributed to Polygnotus, c.440 B.C. Theseus fighting the Amazons (p. 12). Given by Arthur Evans (G.290)

Pl. 7 a,b   Four Tarentine didrachms: *a.* obverse, horseman; *b.* reverse, Taras, the legendary founder of Tarentum, riding on a dolphin. Evans Periods II-IV, c.400-330 B.C. (p. 12). Heberden Coin Room, Ashmolean Museum

23

PLATES

Pl. 8 a,b   Enlarged impressions of Minoan seals, agate (p. 13): a. Middle Minoan, a bull at a cistern and a vaulting acrobat (1938.964): b. Late Minoan, a bull-leaping scene (1938.1079)

Pl. 9 a,b   Enlarged impressions of Late Minoan seals, Spartan basalt (p. 13): a. Minoan genius leading a bull (1938.1040): b. A man-bull (1938.1071) from the Psychro Cave

Pl. 10   Arthur Evans and Duncan Mackenzie watching workmen at the South Dump at Knossos in 1900 (p. 13)

Pl. 11   Arthur Evans standing in the Throne Room, Knossos, in 1900 (p. 13)

Pl. 12   The restored Throne Room at Knossos (p. 15)

Pl. 13   Excavating the bathroom in the Residential Quarter, Knossos, in 1902 (p. 13)

Pl. 14   Excavating the Temple Tomb, Knossos, in 1931 (p. 13,15)

Pl. 15   Arthur Evans, Theodore Fyfe and Duncan Mackenzie at Knossos (p. 13)

Pl. 16   Left: Early Minoan III spouted vase with light on dark decoration (AE.749). Centre: Late Minoan II stirrup jar decorated with an octopus (1910.184). Right: Middle Minoan bridge-spouted jar with spiky wreath pattern and bands of dots (AE.912). All from Knossos (p. 13)

Pl. 17   Late Minoan I pithos from West Magazine X (AE.1126), Knossos (p. 13)

Pl. 18   Pithoi *in situ* in West Magazines XI and XII at Knossos (p. 13)

Pl. 19 a-d   Linear B clay tablets from Knossos (p. 13): a. List of women workers (1910.218): b. Ideogram, sheep (1938.850): c. Cattle inventory (1910.212): d. Armoury, chariot-wheels (1910.211)

Pl. 20   The Villa Ariadne, Knossos, under construction in 1906. It was designed by Christian Doll as an excavation house for Arthur Evans (p. 13)

Pl. 21   Fragment of a fresco (AE.1708) from the Court of the Stone Spout, Palace of Knossos. A girl athlete bull-jumping (p. 14)

Pl. 22   Jarn Mound (p. 15) with pond in the foreground (*Jarn Mound*, pl. 11, facing p. 17)

Pl. 23   Sir Arthur Evans at Youlbury (p. 15). Lord Hampton, who opened the Training Centre for Scout leaders in 1927, sits on his right

PLATE 2

PLATE 3

PLATE 4

PLATE 5

PLATE 6

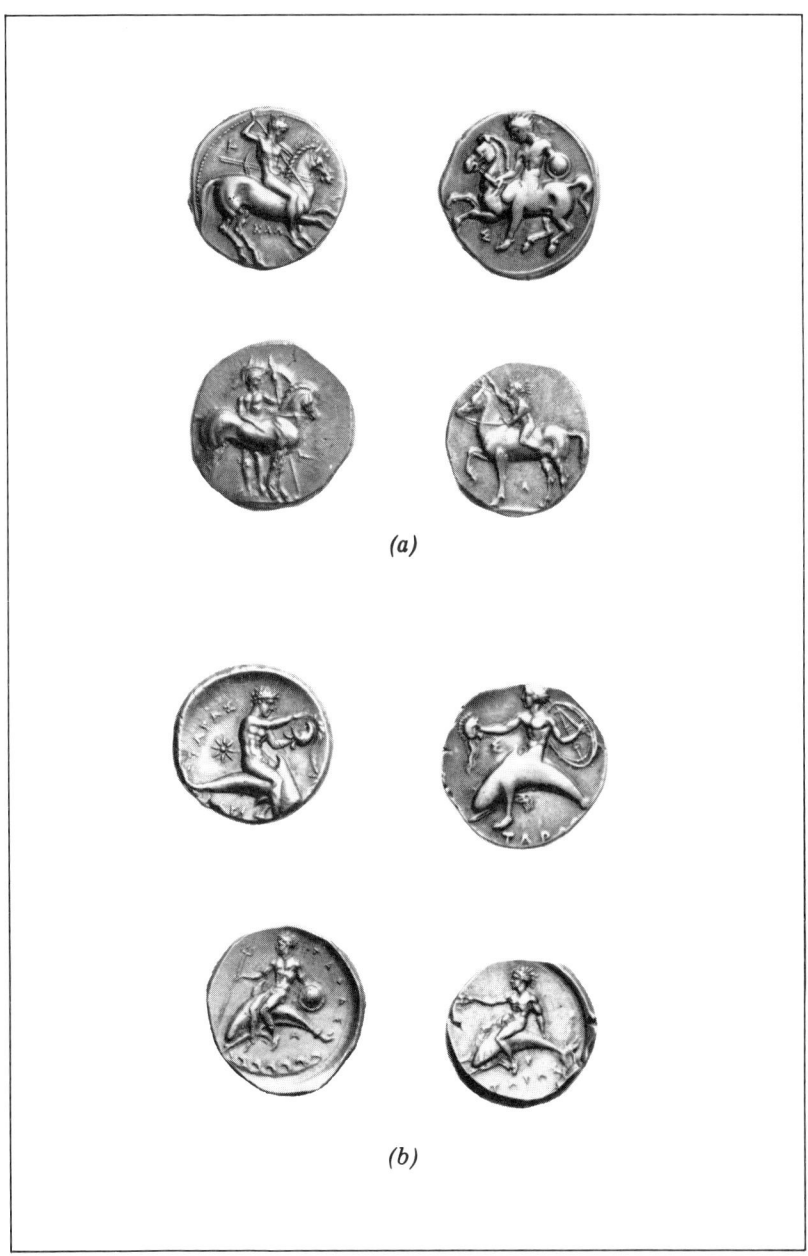

(a)

(b)

PLATE 8

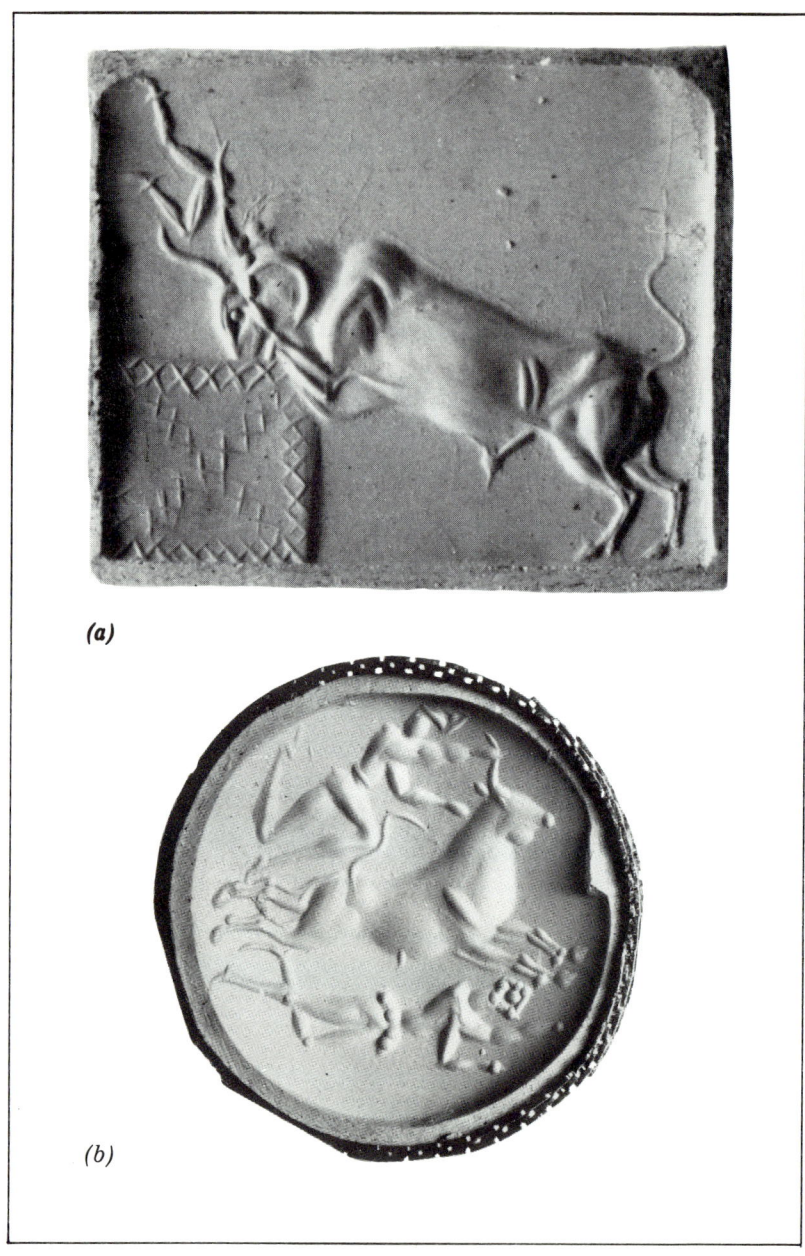

(a)

(b)

PLATE 9

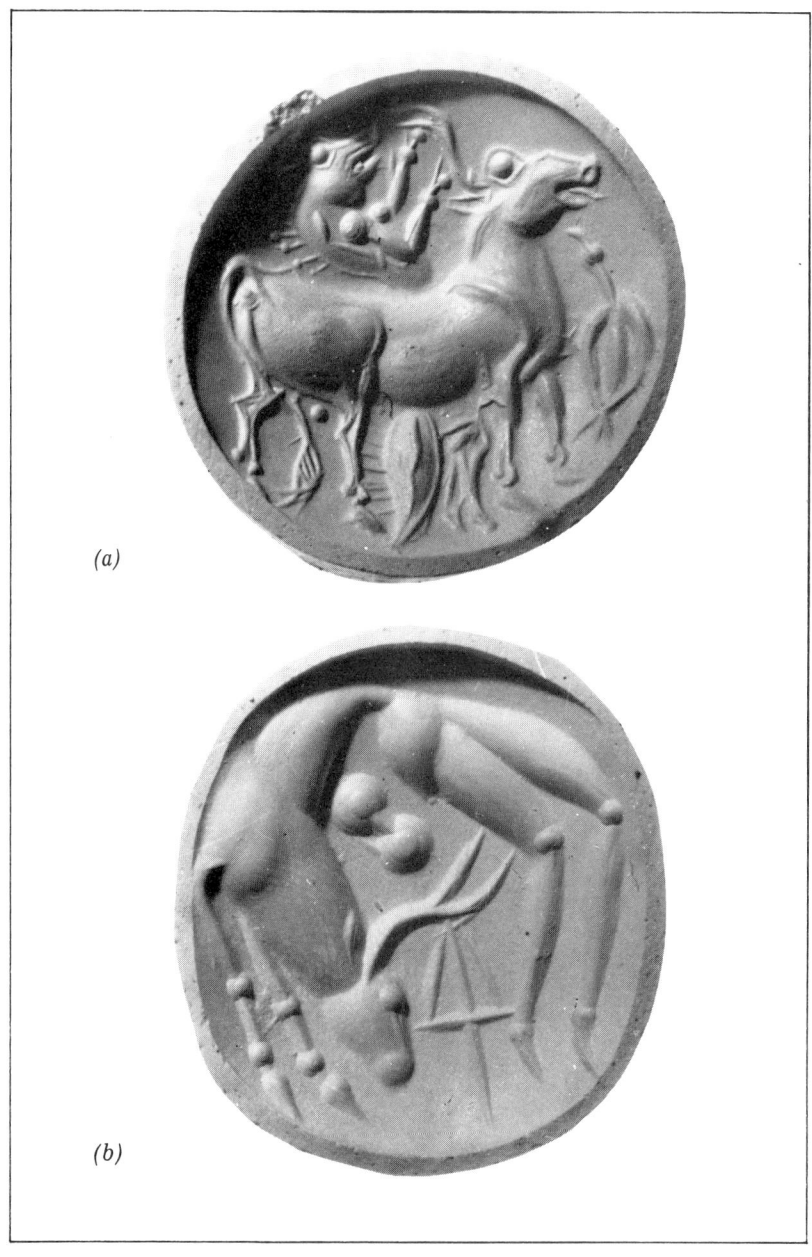

(a)

(b)

PLATE 10

PLATE 11

PLATE 12

PLATE 13

PLATE 14

PLATE 15

PLATE 16

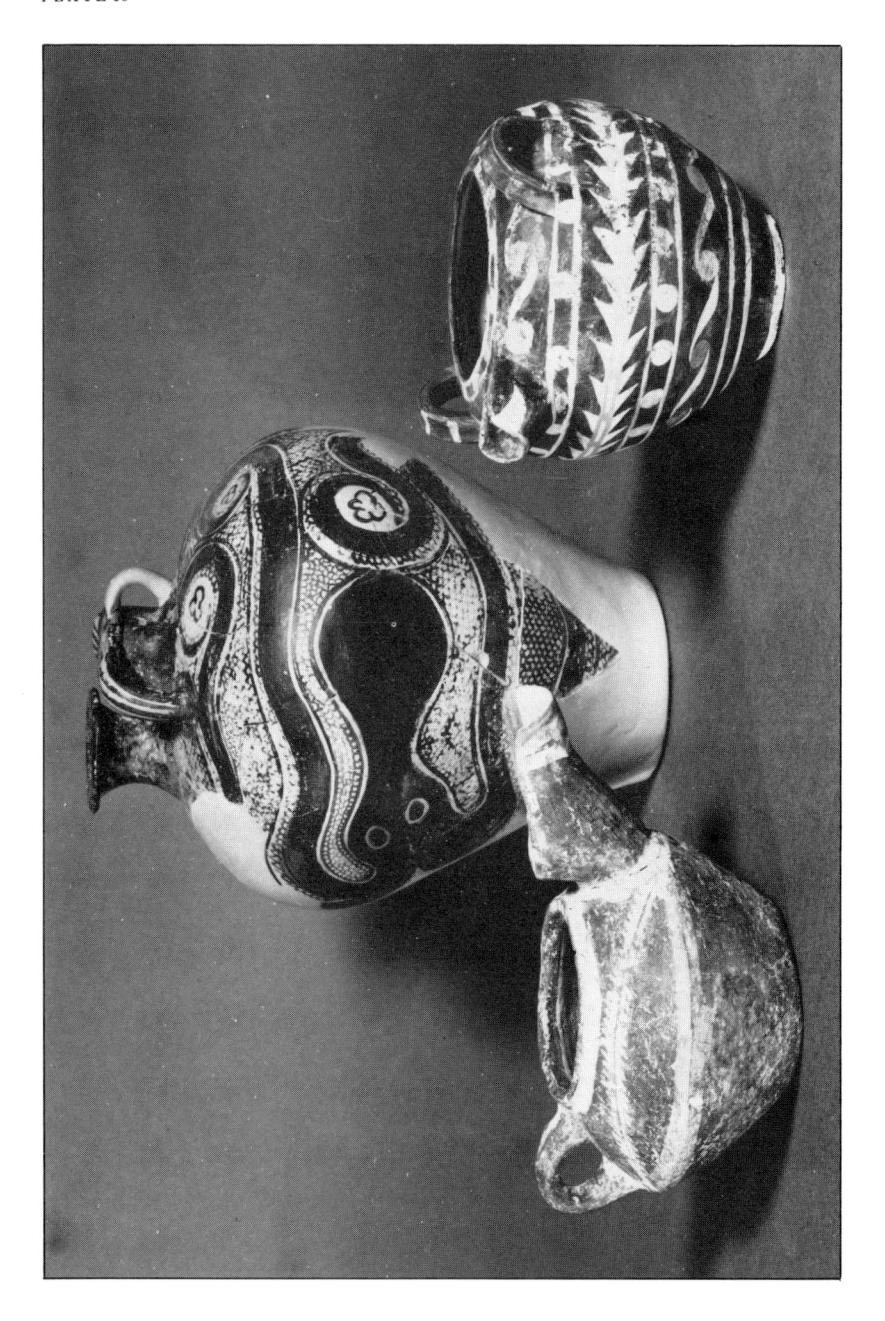

PLATE 17

PLATE 18

PLATE 19

PLATE 20

PLATE 21

PLATE 22

PLATE 23